What Matters The Most

And A Few Other Subtle Lessons Of Life!

By
MARK FIERLE

What Matters The Most
And a Few other Subtle Lessons of Life!
© 2024 Mark Fierle
All rights reserved

ISBN: 979-8-9864517-6-3

First edition printed September 2024
Published by Solutions Press

All rights reserved. Except as permitted by applicable copyright laws, no part of this book may be reproduced, duplicated, sold or distributed in any form or by any means, either mechanical, by photocopy, electronic, or by computer, or stored in a database or retrieval system, without the express written permission of the publisher, except for brief quotations by reviewers.

Printed in the United States of America

This is a work of non-fiction. The ideas presented are those of the author alone. All references to possible results discussed in this book relate to specific past examples and are not necessarily representative of any future results specific individuals may achieve.

Table of Contents

Introduction v
Where Do Smarts Come In? 1
Choices 5
Following The Crowd 9
The Jigsaw Puzzle Of Life 11
Crisis 13
The Excitement Of Life 16
Where Does Our Faith Come From? 17
What Is Courage? 21
What Are You Going To Do For The Rest Of Your Life? 25
Judgmental 27
Forgiveness 31
Whatever Happened To The American Dream? 33
Crisis In Our Schools 37
Education 41
Another Memorable Day With My Dad 43
Updates 51
Human Nature 59
Happiness And Joy 63
What's Happening Today? 67
Risk Taking, A Key To Good Decisions 69
More To Come 73
The Girl With The Green Eyes And A Heart Of Gold 77
A Knock On The Side Of The Head 85
Summary 88
Getting To Know Mark Fierle 89

Introduction

If you ask just about anyone you will most likely get a different response from each. You see we all have different values in life.

Over the course of my research on just what matters the most, it seems for each person interviewed the answers are all different. We also discussed why their answers are all different.

As a result, I came up with the material for this book along the way and have included several other writings, some dating back over forty years and still applicable today.

What I've found is that most of us don't think too much about what's most important except daily things like I've got to take a shower or I'm hungry and got to get some food or the darn traffic is so bad, even what do I have to do to get a raise, innocuous things like these.

My hope is after reading all I've put together you will give this subject some serious thought {not that you haven't already}.

If you are like me, my outlook has changed over the years. Believe the reason for this is what we may call "the face of personality."

That is as we age or mature our personality and outlook changes or at least modifies a bit. Maybe just a little. What do you think?

Now let's get into it. First, we talk about feelings and here's the question, why do smart people do stupid things?

What does smart mean? My interpretation: smart does not make for a fertile mind, and it does not include being stupid. A fertile mind only makes for the possibility that we can be both smart and stupid at the same time. That does not mean only smart people can be stupid. Unfortunately, we all have that gene. However, we often wonder why a smart person at times makes such stupid decisions. That is, the type of decision that ordinary people would never even consider.

So where does stupid come from? Probably several different places. Here are a few but they are not the only ones:

How about being lazy and only going so far when considering an issue. Laziness is possibly the biggest reason for stupid decisions as most of us have that affliction.

Guess that's just part of human nature. We all are blessed with that trait to an extent. Of course, some more than others. Unfortunately, many of these may include our bosses, politicians, even other highly recognized so-called leaders and professors or other experts. Being lazy leads a person no matter how smart to only consider one alternative to an issue instead of the other options. Generally, there is more than one right answer.

Other than lazy, how about greed? Ever heard of making a decision that seems too good to be true? Then of course it really is.

We then rue the fact wondering how could we be so stupid? Yes, greed is one of the seven deadly sins and could be one of the reasons for stupid decisions.

While greed is not a good trait, it often leads to stupidity. Now that does not include ambition and a desire to better oneself through persistence and hard work. At times we plan well, work hard and still we don't reach our goals through no fault of our own. Just bad timing often leads to bad decisions.

Here's another one: how about procrastination. It's not only stupid people that are procrastinators but let's not exclude so-called smart people from that category. Putting things off till tomorrow rather than doing it today can lead to unfavorable results. No matter who is the culprit, that bad word stupid generally fits the bill.

Then there is that thing called attitude. We all have one and we are all known for the one that occupies our brain. At times smart people that make stupid decisions think they know it all. With a know-it-all attitude success becomes very limited or at least brief.

Here is a brief more on attitude.

Both attitude and motivation are two of the most important characteristics of successful people. Have you ever been around someone that perpetually seems to have an "attitude?" I guess we all have at one time or another. Just seems they are always angry or complaining or whatever.

Very seldom do they have a good word to say about anything- unless it's about them. When we talk about our lives and interests in my estimation attitude and motivation go together.

Along this line, negative is the key word. Here is an example, and after it I will ask you a question.

First there was Dr. Norman Vincent Peale, who a number of years ago wrote a book titled *The Power of Positive Thinking*. It is still a bestseller today after 50+ years. Dr. Peale made millions with this concept.

Now for your question: Have you ever known of a best-selling book based on a concept of "negative" thinking? I think not. Here are a few suggestions for helping ourselves and others with this thing called attitude:
- Work on it all the time
- Achievers motivate others with a positive attitude
- Negative attitudes create anger and depression. Who needs more of that?
- Attitude and motivation are the first order of importance, brains are secondary!

As the old song from the 60's goes ...
"Accentuate the positive ,
 eliminate the negative
 and don't mess with Mister in between..."

Getting back. There are many other reasons why smart people make stupid decisions from time to time or more frequently. Here's a consideration {and probably a lot of others} have observed many people seem smart and see the problem but aren't wise enough to solve the problem.

In my opinion, a smart person is wise enough to solve the problem. Perhaps that is the difference. Naturally, as opinions go the old saying "the lion doesn't care about the lamb's opinion."

Being both smart and wise is a gift.

The one thing that hasn't been discussed yet is the question: is STUPIDITY REVERSIBLE?

Let's hope to some extent it is, however, it only is if the person making stupid decisions or doing stupid things realizes what they are getting themselves into and maybe why. Or we can put it another way. How about are we lazy? What if we have been like this all our lives and have gotten away with it most of the time, maybe that's just the way I am.

If that is the case and that person does not want to put in the effort to improve unless something hits them upside the head no matter how smart they are, unless it is meaningful that change will not get rid of most stupidity. What do you think?

Okay enough about stupidity and stupid decisions. Let's get on to a different topic. What I mean is this is a topic that seems to have been going on in today's world and has been going on for the past 20 or so years and no one has an answer. The topic or issue is compromise.

In today's world compromise seems impossible. It's almost like there are only two sides, almost like two fighters in a ring and there is only going to be one winner. Kind of like the other party is wrong and the situation is hopeless. This seems prevalent in today's political community and that's a shame. It also trickles down to our everyday lives and can lead to divisions between family and friends. However, the political community is not the only culprit, there's the Educational community that used to promote "thinking" as one of its main reasons to get a higher education. Whereas brainwashing now in many of our elite universities is its major feature.

These aren't the only areas where chasms have arisen but when you think about it take our political leaders as an example. They are supposed to be the deal makers but how can they do that when a compromise is off the table?

Think about it, how can we make our own deals without compromise? After all, don't we compromise everyday whether it be with our spouse, children, boss, fellow employees or maybe the used car salesman?

How did we get to this point? Can this trend be reversed? Can't we all just get along? After all, the future wellbeing of our country and our persona is what matters the most.

Here's an idea, how about what if it was not my way or your way but a third way? The third way being a best unifying way. The only thing being you would need the opposing parties to agree when critical differences occur and one of the parties asks - would you be willing to work with me to create a solution that is better than what either of us have now? Believe this can work again every day with us personally.

Now this is just one solution, and we know that conflict is going to be with us probably forever more. Today's social media, 24-hour news cycle, polarizing activity groups etc. will see to that. However, by creating positive energy and eliminating a winner and loser atmosphere good solutions can be worked out.

A few things can help, for example beware of "pride, it is a divider.

Be a lifelong learner. You will be surprised.

One thing I have advocated in all my books is to make some quiet time to think through your decisions and problems. I have been told that quiet music, a glass of wine and no interruptions can be a real stimulant for the brain cells. Try it, you will like it!

When you are discussing a difference with a colleague or opponent a suggestion is to be enthusiastic and relentless in finding a "win" for them. Wins are infectious and chances are they will endeavor to find the same for you.

Where Do Smarts Come In?

This is a question that often comes up in young people, not so much in the older generation. How smart do I have to be?

I've written about this subject in previous books but thought it could be expanded on a bit in this book as it's one of the things we think about from time to time. It's also one of the things that matter the most.

For example, I wish I had more brains. Or wish I was smarter. Or how come I don't get that algebra stuff?

Let's look at it a little differently.

The first item is what is your IQ? That is a tough one. You see when I was asked this question I was perplexed. At some time, I must have known but to tell the truth I have no clue. Do you?

When researching this subject of IQ, I was interested in determining how our personal IQ was in the overall scope of things.

While it can be important this is what I found, including a couple of interesting facts.

Here's one, when IQ {Intelligence Quotient} was established, it was done for schools not to find out who were the smartest, but which students needed special educational help. Didn't realize that.

What does it mean anyhow?

- Does it tell how smart we are? If so, how smart are we? My answer is probably smarter than some but dumber than a whole lot more.

- Does it tell how good of a person we are? I think not.
- Does it tell how much common sense we have? I don't think so.
- Does it tell how good of a decision maker we are? How can it? It hasn't experienced any of our decisions
- Does it tell our level of our motivation and attitude, how we react to bad or difficult times, our diligence, moral equivalency, cognitive ability or social skills? I don't think so.

As kids much seems to have been made by our parents of their kids' IQ. This is nice when we are going to school but not much after we are out in the real world for some time.

Actually, it was important to my mom when she went to her Bridge club and she could say, oh my son tested out at near genius! Give me a break.

History however is replete with examples of high achievers that were not known for their brilliance.

Some include General and President Ulyess S. Grant who finished near the bottom of his class at West Point yet out-generaled and defeated Robert E. Lee, the man thought to be the greatest General of his time.

Then there was Ronald Reagan, that actor from California.

How about Abraham Lincoln, the rail splitter from Illinois.

Next is Winston Churchill who was thought to be a nincompoop by many but, we all would be repressed and speaking German if it wasn't for his leadership. His predecessor, Neville Chamberlain was hoodwinked by Hitler.

We can go on and on to illustrate many more overachievers not considered brilliant.

Then its not hard to find many smart derelicts on the streets of our major cities

What I'm getting at is, "It's what you do with what you've got and not necessarily how smart you are." I think that was from either Benjamin Franklin or Thomas Jefferson.

I was told a long time ago that guarding your attitude is the greatest influence on a person's conduct. You keep working on yours and I will keep working on mine. And you know we'll both win!

Choices

What Matters the Most comes next. We can discuss what the most important issues in our life are right now. After all, as time goes by the issues may change. Let's call this "the jigsaw puzzle of life." We'll get to that shortly.

In life we make choices, generally ones that are easy to live with. We can say life is a matter of choices. However, choices also have consequences. Now what I mean is "feelings" are not choices, actions are!

Most choices made by young children come from our parents or guardians. They teach us the elementary essentials in order that we become self-sufficient or damage ourselves. Then we go to school where we are taught how to read, write and add and subtract, etc. plus social interaction. This generally enables us to get along in the world.

As young people, most of these choices are not ours to make. It seems the most important issues during this stage are from our parents or others that influence our everyday life. These include our teachers, maybe the swim coach, our piano teacher or maybe even our babysitters and the kids our mother allows us to get together with, etc. Most of these we have little say in selecting.

Growing older we get to make more choices. For example, as boys and girls we may want to participate in certain sports, dance, music, church and a host of other activities. Many of these lead to the initial changes to our outlook on life. We've got a long way to go from here, but these activities can lead to happiness or sadness in our short lives.

Along the way we learn about mistakes, especially since we all tend to make our share. Now here's the deal, when you make too many or they are egregious, they may even be called or considered "DOOZIES." With that a whole other concept comes into play.

Let's say you make many or they are doozies. There is the chance you will be known as a "DOOFUS." believe me, who wants to be called a doofus?

When that happens and we are known in that context, how do we feel about ourselves? There is a good chance we will stop believing in our ability to do the right thing. That means we stop believing in ourselves. What a horrible thought.

Then you do the "right thing" even though others think you are CRAZY! What a way to go.

Here's my thought, we can all learn from our mistakes, no matter how many we make or how old we are.

As a suggestion, especially for parents, guardians and grandparents, when we are in the criticizing mode be patient and don't over criticize but be understanding and listen. Maybe you will learn something. After all, how many of us as either in our youth or as we got older, made doozie type mistakes? Probably more than once.

If we can talk it out and discuss choices that can be good or not so good and teach the difference, perhaps that person will learn. After all, you have the experience. With guidance we can all make better choices. Just make sure we realize there are consequences. In fact, I'm going to talk to myself about this subject because I don't know how many times I have been a DOOFUS! Don't ask my wife, she'll say plenty.

Let's go on. Many times, as we morph into the middle stages of our short time here on Earth, we begin to associate with kids that can become our lifelong friends or buddies. This is true with both boys and girls. It is also a time that can be very instrumental in our development. This is called the "comparison complex" What is this phenomenon you ask?

It hits all of us and often lasts our entire lives. How we handle it can have a great impact on how we eventually make it through.

As such some of the biggest influences are the people we hang out with as kids.

Seems while we are in school, we want to be accepted as part of the group.

I can remember as a thirteen-year-old being considered an outsider. You see, as a boy from what was considered the country {actually the suburbs} and going to high school in the city there was a big difference.

One day in my freshman year a fellow freshman tried to pick a fight with me. I have no idea why. We couldn't go at it on the school grounds but arranged to meet in the adjoining cemetery grounds after school. So, we did. Only problem, he brought five of his homeboy buddies with him as backup. Whoa, I was greatly outnumbered.

We went at it for a while, neither of us did much damage to the other. Probably a good thing I didn't kick his butt maybe even backed down when I saw the odds, or I could have been greatly damaged.

The thing was I stood up to him and his buddies even though I was outnumbered.

Point being after it was all over, we shook hands and over time he and his buddies became some of my best high school friends. We have remained so even as we went our separate ways over the years.

Goes to show you.

Following The Crowd

When it comes to comparison, we all, especially at a young age, want to be a part of the "in crowd." This is apparent for girls that must have the right clothes etc. For boys it's being a member of the right gang.

As we grow older it's like keeping up with the Jones's. This can be a real problem for some of us. That is, when our neighbor or colleague gets a nicer car or buys a nicer house in a better neighborhood. Then we must match what they have even if we are putting ourselves in financial jeopardy. What happens when the bottom falls out or we have a setback? Life is not a one-way street, we all know it has a lot of curves and potholes.

I wrote in one of my previous books about a colleague of my son-in-law who is a police officer, one of L.A.'s finest. He grew up in Santa Ana, CA near a noted violent gang area.

One day while in high school he and some of his friends were girl chasing, something common among teenagers. Martin and one of his friends decided rather than doing that they would go to a movie.

As it turned out that was a fortunate choice as his other buddies didn't realize the girls they were chasing were gang girls and their gang members came by and did a drive-by shooting wounding several of Martin's friends.

Martin never joined a gang. My point is: Following the crowd is one thing but be mindful of the people in that crowd. They can have a great influence on your life now and in the future.

Don't know whether Martin got lucky that day and made the right choice. We make choices every day. Some are good, some not so good and hopefully we learn from our mistakes or bad choices.

What if we don't get what we think we want the most? How about the things that really count like health, family, friends or just people that we love or love us.

Here's a suggestion: give yourself a break. What do you do when you need to relax or get in a better mood? If you are like my wife, nothing makes her feel better than something as simple as getting a pedicure. How about you?

The Jigsaw Puzzle Of Life

There can be many pieces to a jigsaw puzzle, it seems the more difficult ones have many more than the easier ones. At least that has always been the way it is with me. While I like to do multi-piece puzzles, most of them take me a long time to complete.

Yet I know a couple of people can do the puzzles that take me a year to finish in an hour or less. How the heck they do it is beyond me.

I do know that when a more complicated puzzle is finished my level of happiness and satisfaction is greater by far than when I complete an easier puzzle.

Oh well, maybe that's just like life. Some of us make the complicated things of life simple and for others the simple things complicated.

Guess we should consider that simple things are not necessarily easy and may take a long time to figure out. For example, think about the wheel. The wheel is a simple thing but, what did they do before the wheel?

All they could do was drag their burden. Sounds easy huh? How about building the pyramids and dragging those multi-ton stones? Again, not easy. After the wheel it became much simpler and easier.

Now if our goal is to make things simpler and thus easier, that may be a task that has some complications. Chances are it may take more than just a few tries. May even take years to figure out. For example, again take the wheel , it was not invented and utilized until about 3500 BC. That is somewhere between the Neolithic and Bronze age. They say the reason it took so long was that it was not part of nature.

It also needed an axle to make it work. Once that was figured out it was simple.

The same goes for us. Our complications may take some time, even years to simplify. Once we get there, however, it will probably seem simple. We may even think, why didn't I think of that before?

Another part of the jigsaw puzzle of life is "what is the picture of success?" There seems to be so many misconceptions. In fact, if you ask several people what their idea of success is you will most likely get that many different responses.

Now I don't want to give you an answer but from my point of view it goes like this. Could it be like being on a bicycle? A bicycle only keeps upright when it is moving forward toward something. For us it's the same, this is our poise and equilibrium.

If we are not moving forward, we are either standing still, moving backward or falling on our butt. Seems all our life we are engineered to work toward a goal. For the most part when we have a goal we are at our happiest. Working toward something like a goal is what it's all about. That goal may be very simple, like improving my golf scores or getting better at making a tasty omelet, even taking 5000+ steps everyday. I don't know about you but, that's how it is for me. My suggestion then is to keep from being an old fogey and make good goals. No matter what your age, always have a goal. It will keep you on your toes all your given days. Oh, success to me is satisfaction. When we achieve a goal not only do we have a feeling of success but of happiness and satisfaction. Will be talking about this subject in a later chapter.

Crisis

Did you ever wonder why in the military new recruits go through months of Basic Training? Well, it's quite simple. No, it's not, Not only do they learn to march, obey orders, self defense and shoot a gun at a target, they are not under pressure when they learn to do these military type tasks. For example, if they are tasked with shooting at a target during target practice and they miss, they get to do it over until they get it right.

Nobody shoots back at them or otherwise threatens their wellbeing other than the drill sergeant.

The result of all this repetition is muscle memory. When they get in the line of battle and the enemy is shooting at them and threatening the wellbeing of not only themselves but their fellow soldiers, muscle memory comes into being.

They then react in a positive manner without having to think about what they must do. This is true especially if they are well trained and muscle memory counts.

Here are a few examples:

A fine golfer friend of mine once told me his secret when I asked him how he got to be such a fine golfer. He said the more he practiced it seemed the better he got. What he of course meant was that by practicing he learned muscle memory. This muscle memory came into play when he was in a high-pressure situation on the golf course.

Here's another one, Mike Trout, one of the best baseball players in the Major Leagues, always makes it a practice to take the first pitch while at bat. It doesn't matter how tempting the pitch is, he doesn't swing. Why is that? After all Ted Williams, probably one of the greatest all-time hitters, used to say, hit the first good pitch. Mike Trout has a different approach in taking the first pitch thrown. There is no pressure. You will be able to watch the pitcher, see how he winds up and how the ball moves. Works for him and reduces the amount of pressure. While this is no crisis, who needs more pressure?

Then there is my son-in-law, Robert Pedregon the Police Officer. You probably read about him in my previous books. By the way he just got promoted to Lieutenant.

About ten years ago as a young police officer at Los Angeles Airport he was instrumental in the take down of a murdering terrorist. This was a true crisis and thanks to great training and practice in handling such an event they got the guy and saved an untold number of lives. Again, practice and training with no pressure helped to create the muscle memory of that fateful day.

Another prime example is after retiring I worked part time at a prime golf course in Orange County. One of my colleagues was a retired Army Colonel from the Vietnam War days. He was a combat veteran with 7 purple hearts and had risen from enlisted man to Colonel.

We were just close to engaging in Desert Storm and I asked him how soldiers felt about a pending conflict of this nature? He thought for a moment and had a simple three-word reply, "It's party time."

I asked him, "Holy smokes why?"

Again, he replied, "This is what we trained for."

As we wrap up this segment, here is what a crisis is all about in my way of thinking: A crisis leads to excitement vs. fear. Too much excitement then leads to fear. Now, do you think all those soldiers in Desert Storm were thinking it was "party time?" Probably not as too much excitement, I've been told, leads to fear.

The question is how can we turn down excitement yet keep it at a reasonable rate? Probably the best way is to stay within yourself.

To me, one good way is to ask yourself, "What is the worst that can happen?"

When we get through that and figure it out maybe it won't seem the crisis is so bad after all, and we can reduce that excitement and likewise your fear will lessen.

A real crisis will probably need or even require excitement. The question is why and how much. The problem is quite frequently we overestimate how much there is to this so-called crisis. By doing so we can create too much excitement, which leads us to something bad called "the jitters." Have you ever had a case of jitters during a difficult time? I know I have and that's something bad.

As a result, we don't handle the problem in the proper manner and end up harming rather than helping solve the situation, perhaps even leading to disaster. On the other hand, looking at the crisis in a steady manner can lead to our saying it's not that bad! Worry then diminishes and we go on to really working on solving the problem. Remember, just think, "What do I have to lose?"

It's like the salesman who didn't get the order they were counting on. He realizes he can always get another customer or even go back and find out from the original customer what their concerns are and learn from the mistake. Learning from our mistakes is a big deal. Does this make any sense?

The Excitement Of Life

While this section is not about the excitement caused by a crisis, it is about our entire existence. You all know that as we go through our life here on earth there are times when we get very excited and others when just a little bit.

Of course, the "very exciting" times are generally as we experience good times. The question is when does this excitement begin? It starts in my opinion when we are conceived, and it doesn't end when we die! When we die it goes to the next stage of our existence with us.

I won't get too much into this but if you are a believer in God, you realize that as we arrive at the Pearly Gates and are greeted by St. Peter the aura of excitement will probably be at a very high level.

That's well above my pay grade so you can refer to a host of scholars and religious experts for further clarification. Whew, got out of that one but it's a complex subject that really is very simple.

However, over our lifetime excitement levels change for different reasons.

If you think back, how has excitement changed as your life progressed?

Consider some of the highs and lows and recognize as we grow older there will be more of each.

Where Does Our Faith Come From?

Have you ever thought of that or even considered the tenets of a subject like that?

Is it our faith in God that guides us to do the right thing? Or maybe it's something else. What could that be? After all the agonizing.

I'm curious where my faith came from, was it because I went to Catholic schools for sixteen years? I doubt it as for a long time I didn't go to Mass every Sunday as was taught in schools and the church.

That did not mean I was not somewhat spiritual during that period of my life. As a matter of fact, I always prayed to Mary, Mother of God during difficult periods. It always gave me peace.

As I think about where my faith came from my immediate thought probably came from my mom. Reason being that she always told me, "God never gives us more than we can handle."

What did she really mean by that? After all, some only lead a relatively short life with a lot of hard stops along the way. Others have a long pain-free life and others a long painful existence. How can that be fair?

What was she talking about and what did she mean?

I remember someone telling me about life expectancy from a year standpoint. Believe it was Fr. Larry, our parish priest.

When you think about it as we grow older, a year seems like a very short period. Yet in the life of a five-year-old one year is a very long time. He explained that for a five-year-old that is only one fifth of their life, on the other hand for an eighty-year-old it is a very short time as it is one eightieth of their life cycle. That's why to a youngster and an older person one year has a totally different meaning.

The more we think about this there are millions of years before we were conceived and there will be millions of years after we pass from here on earth and go onto the next stage. Again, I ask, "Where does our faith come from? What chapter of our existence?"

Therefore, we live a long or short life, it is only a miniscule part of our existence. Whether I guess what we do here is only a test for what comes next.

If mom was correct when she told me that God never gives us more than we can handle, she meant that our entire existence is in play, and we have the faith to make it.

Of course, how we conduct ourselves here on earth has a great deal to do with our heavenly reward or the next stage of our existence.

Does that make sense?

Maybe the hard times of our life are part of the lessons that God teaches us while we are here.

Perhaps doubting is part of going through those difficulties or declining periods of our life. That does not mean we stop being a good person or at least striving to do good things, especially for others.

Maybe doing some not so good things is part of the lesson of life. After all we are humans and sinners.

Again, I ask where does our faith come from?

Oh , here's another aspect of what faith is about. What about the faith of Muslims, Buddhists, Hindus and the multitude of other religions/ beliefs? Don't they have faith too? Where does it come from? It may be different from the Jewish/ Christian concept but, it's faith nonetheless!

While I think about us humans here on earth and that all are included, there is only one God.

Where do we go from here?

With only one God and many different beliefs do you think He excluded the billions that do not follow our Lord Jesus Christ, son of the Father?

I know Jesus said, referring to his followers, that there is only a narrow gate open to those that want to get to heaven. But didn't Jesus say He loves us all and that is why He died on the cross essentially to forgive our sins and pave our way to heaven? The question is does that mean only those with one select focus who follow the ten commandments, and the eight beatitudes are eligible?

Let's talk about that. It's a deep subject and I don't want you to think that I am a religious zealot, even an expert or religious philosopher, just an ordinary man asking questions. But what do you think?

If you go by Webster's Dictionary the definition of faith states it is the unquestioning belief that does not require proof or evidence. Generally, it is referred to in a Christian religious context.

I'm again curious where it comes from and how it is obtained? This to me is the subject that matters the most. Haven't even talked about the heretics, agnostics, atheists and even those that once had faith, but had it stolen. Let's do it. What about these people? Are they bad folks? I doubt it. But why are they without faith? Perhaps their faith was stolen. If so, what was it that led to stolen faith? Could it be because they are disillusioned?

Some of it may be because they are disappointed. Disappointment can lead to a lot of bad decisions. In fact, it can lead to things that are not in our best interests. We just don't realize it.

Over time we all have disappointments, but they don't necessarily consume our whole life. Here's how we can get over these negatives:

- One way is to not give up. Just figure it out, why are we disappointed?
- Here's another, being disillusioned is a bitch and something that takes time and thought to get over.
- In my case I have been disillusioned many times over the years but, after time and thinking about it I recognized maybe it was my fault to some extent and didn't recognize where I screwed up. Possibly I was naive and didn't realize how naive I was. Note: we are all naive at one time or another, but we should not use it as an excuse.

These are just a couple of thoughts on the subject and are not the end of the discussions. I would really like to hear your thoughts on the subject as it impacts us all at one time or another.

This concept is really beyond my pay grade. I only hope that it opens our minds and gets us thinking about what is important. Peace be with you!

What Is Courage?

Is it only shown by the first responders such as firefighters that go into a burning building? Or the policemen that get up in the morning and go on duty not knowing what they will face that day? How about the soldiers that face an enemy?

These are the ones we ordinarily think of having courage.

However, courage is not limited to these everyday individuals. Let's look at the rest of us and ask how we determine how courageous we can be? Afterall most of us think we are just "ordinary people."

My wife, for example, watching a military themed movie says, "I'm glad I'm not a man as I couldn't do that!"

Of course, not only men are soldiers, firefighters or police officers.

Let's look at it from a different perspective. How about the wife of that soldier, police officer or firefighter who manages the family and sends her spouse off on those dangerous assignments not knowing from day to day if she will get notification that something bad happened to her loved one. If that is not courage personally, I don't know what is.

Going a step further, what about the ordinary wife of an ordinary man with an ordinary job just trying to make a living for his family who unexpectedly gets laid off? Does that make her less than courageous when she comforts her husband by giving him support, telling him don't worry, we'll get through this difficult time.

Even in the inflationary times of today with the price of gasoline and groceries, etc. going sky high. Ordinary folks can find it very difficult to manage their lives. Yes, this takes courage. Let's just keep in mind there are a lot of charitable people and organizations like churches in our communities that are dedicated to helping those in need. It is not hopeless.

Regarding inflation, let's just pray that contrary to the late 70's and mid 80's we don't get accustomed to these difficult times and take it for granted that this is just the way it is. What can we then do about it? That's a whole different subject but here's one thing: plant a Square Foot Garden.

It's amazing how much you can grow in a small space. Maybe even all the vegetables that you are currently paying an arm and a leg for on a weekly basis. Not only that but it's easy, cheap and anyone can do it. As a Master Gardener and Certified Square Foot Garden Teacher, while living in California I taught thousands of prospective people the tenets of how to do it. Don't worry, all over the world folks are learning how to feed themselves. I remember when the Foundation asked me to teach a group of students from the University of California going to Rwanda to help the citizens learn how to grow their own veggies.

Seems one of their biggest problems was that if they had their own garden, when the crops ripened, they would have them stolen before they could harvest them. I taught them to use a two-foot by three-foot raised bed either on wheels or with a slide feature and drag the small bed into their homes at night when thievery would generally occur. Note: when the students returned, they told me that the system was well received. They even sent me a DVD with examples. I also did a similar project for an American teacher working in Haiti after the earthquake a few years ago. Here in the

USA, I also worked as a volunteer with The Braille Institute to teach the visually impaired how they could grow their own vegetable garden. That also was a very interesting and heart-worthy project.

If you would like to learn more, check online with the Square Foot Garden Foundation.

What I'm trying to say here is that courage has many faces and from time to time we are all on the firing line. What matters the most is that Our Dear God has given us the ability to muddle thru and not give up hope. Keep the faith and don't give up HOPE.

Here's an example of a person who did keep the faith and didn't give up hope. It comes from my book entitled *What Comes Next*.

In that book I wrote a chapter entitled Miracles. Now miracles are something that were more prevalent a couple of thousand years ago before the age of Christ. But miracles still occur today, we just don't always recognize them. Often, we think it's just a coincidence or we were just lucky.

In this case a good friend of mine Jim Ryan had bought this book and after reading it sent it to the wife of a dear friend whose husband was suffering from terminal cancer. It seems the doctors had done everything possible, and the wife had given up hope. She read the book and reread it as something caught her eye. Now this was during the heaviest stages of the pandemic, and I had written that it seemed strange washing our hands with soap and water had been as good at stopping the virus spreading as the vaccines. What I wrote was " doctors treat but God cures," almost like a miracle.

Now this lady was a Christian but had stopped practicing and going to church for a few years. After reading this she thought and began praying and asking God for help in curing her beloved husband.

Guess what. Jim got a call from her, and she told him that her husband had been cured with no sign of terminal cancer. Now I don't know if this was a miracle, but he is still healthy and alive. As an author that touched someone, you don't know how that made me feel. My goal here is to just say don't give up hope and ask God for help.

Having courage is something big and we need to recognize we all have it in one way or another.

What Are You Going To Do For The Rest Of Your Life?

Have you ever asked yourself that question? Guess it comes down to choices. Some choices can be good and some not so good. In fact, choices can have a great impact on the outlook we have. From here it is the happiness, satisfaction or even sadness that occurs in our entire short period here on earth.

Have you ever thought about who gave you the inspiration to love, do the right thing, work hard, help others, give to others, have fun, be a good person, even led you in the wrong direction? Who made you happy, gave you hope or pissed you off?

Here's a bit more when it comes to life.

It is said you only experience more happiness when you are confronted with more life. This becomes more living, more accomplishments, more setbacks, more loving. Attain more of your goals. These are things that lead us to appreciate the good parts of life.

The longer we live the more setbacks and mistakes come our way. But the ones that have happiness never give up.

Another channel of happiness is when others help us and we help others, especially as we grow older.

These are factors that influence our everyday being and it's good to think about those that have influenced us from time to time.

We can also look at it from a different perspective. After all who have we done all these things to? Who do we influence? Who has influenced us?

Influence is what we either give to others or get from others. Even the things we watch on TV have an influence on our outlook.

Possibly you may recall the chapter in my book called "brainwashing 101" written by my contributing author John Pedroarena, It talks about how TV ads go about the brainwashing that is done by the ad men on Madison Avenue.

As John says in his chapter, who wants our brains to be controlled by young upstart advertising moguls?

While I certainly do not want to disparage the advertising world and many of the fine companies that use them to promote their products, after all they spend millions of dollars in this endeavor.

My reason for bringing this up is to just remind us all how powerful they and we are as an "influence" in all our lives. Whether we are spending millions for promotion purposes or just with our actions.

Judgmental

What a thing to talk about. Why should we, you say?

Well for one thing we are all judgmental in many ways. Do you think you are not judgmental as most of us consider ourselves not to be so?

However, most of us are, even if we don't admit it.

Let's look at it this way, ever since being born we are taught to be judgmental.

First, it's our parents that tell us what we can and cannot do, who we can hang out with and who we cannot hang out with along with much of the same. Next, it's our schoolteachers who tell us how to do things and make us memorize all those rote things like arithmetic tables and the ABC's.

This called structure and being judgmental should lead to our ability in making improvements and worthy changes through our learned ability to think. By thinking we become judgmental. That is, what we like or don't approve of.

Often our judgements are greatly influenced by others as to what is good, bad or indifferent. This is where we must be diligent. Here is an example:

Think of this when it comes to good or bad judgements. What if a so-called bad or perceived bad person came up to you while being out in the desert. You were very thirsty and just wanted a cool drink of water. Cool clear water!

Then this so-called or perceived bad person saw your need and offered you a cool clear drink of water. What would you do? Think about that.

My point is to be careful how you judge people. Often, we judge others based on acts we think they have either committed or others have told us they committed. It can be the way they look, dress, of a different race even if they are fat, too old or too young. How about social status, political beliefs and on and on.

Look at it like the Jews did Jesus. This was about the times the "well off" Jews known as the Pharisees castigated Him while He was preaching to the downtrodden and the so-called bad people of the day. Oh, He was castigated because they thought He was preaching to the wrong people.

They thought Jesus should have been preaching to them and not to the ones that really needed it. This created jealousy on their part and may have even led them to demand from Pontius Pilate when they were asked, what we should do with this King of the Jews? and their response was "crucify Him."

They judged wrong, the real people that needed help were the people being spoken to and He was telling them why. Unfortunately, the Pharisees of the time did not see it that way. Why did Jesus do this? Namely because he loves all of us human beings and wants all of us to enjoy heavenly rewards. By speaking and giving parables and performing miracles that the people of that time could see and understand He could influence not only them but, hoards of others.

Making mistakes while judging is an everyday occurrence for all of us. Not all are big mistakes. My suggestion is to just be judicious.

Again, just because they think or look different than us does not condemn them as bad people. After all, each of us has our own different beliefs and standards. Think of this, we are all human beings created and loved by God. None of us are perfect, except for you and me and I'm not so sure about you! {just kidding}.

PS: My reference to Our Lord Jesus Christ was not meant to be a religious dialogue but just an example that we are all aware of. After all God said, "He is my son in whom I'm well pleased."

Here are a few thoughts:
- Learn from our mistakes or misconceptions. Our mistakes or misconceptions teach us. We should learn from them. Keep in mind just as a Masterpiece is perfection, we are not. If we were there would be nothing else. Unfortunately, we are not Masterpieces, just ask Adam and Eve.
- Be forgiving. It is peaceful and don't we need more peace?
- Try to do the right thing, especially to others that are not the same as us.
- Try to be understanding. That can take a great effort. Not all of us will make that effort but the ones that do will gain the rewards.

Now this has been just a short excerpt but, let me ask you a question, would you accept that glass of cool, clear water that the so-called bad man offered to you while you were thirsty. The American Dream. Where has it gone? Hmmm.

The next couple of chapters are completely off the topics discussed so far in this book. Will be getting back shortly. They still are a part of What Matters the Most.

Perhaps they were included because while we change over the years, for the most part our prime values stay with us. They are talks I gave over forty years ago and I was fascinated when I found them. The reason they were included is because I felt they are relevant even today. I will be interested in hearing what you think. Good or bad!

Before we get to these here is one more thought for the day.

Forgiveness

Forgiveness is a very interesting word. Think about it.

What if you had a difficult time forgiving someone that did a wrong that did not harm you and if they said they were sorry and promised not to do it again?

Where does forgiveness begin and end? How does it affect your outlook on life?

Holding a grudge can impact our life negatively. If someone did a wrong that did not harm you, would you forgive them?

Forgiveness is a virtue and is different than just not liking that person. As I've heard people say, they like whisky, cigars and maybe three people! Oh, that was probably me. I like a lot more than three people.

Being non-forgiving can be about creating emotional scars unless we have "thick skin." The problem here is if we have too thick of a skin, we never get to experience the joys of the everyday world.

Here is another perspective as forgiveness is not always about forgiving others. Often it is about forgiving ourselves.

For many it is at least as hard as doing the same for others.

Why is that? While I don't really know, I have been told its guilt that hangs with us. Maybe it would be better if we forgave ourselves and gave up the guilt of our past indiscretions. Let's make a pact to forgive not only others but ourselves. The next couple of chapters are completely off the topics discussed so far in this book. Will be getting back shortly. They still are a part of What Matters the Most.

Perhaps they were included as while we change over the years for the most part our prime values stay with us. They are talks I gave over forty years ago and I was fascinated when they were found .The reason they were included is because I felt they are relevant even today. I would be interested in hearing what you think. Good or bad!

Not that forgiveness is necessarily an easy task. Even Jesus, while on the cross, asked his Father, "God, why have you forsaken me?"

We all get hurt sometimes but being able to put it aside and go on with our life makes for a better, happier person. Isn't that one of the things that matters the most?

Whatever Happened To The American Dream?

You know the one I'm talking about; where an American works hard and makes good and is recognized for his/her effort and thrift.
(Note this was written in 1982.)

This concept has been what our forefathers fought for when the Constitution was enacted. Until that is, just a few years ago. We don't seem to know where this dream has gone.

Especially now, with our economy slowed down, and inflation is taking a big bite. Now we are hearing more and more often, "punish those that have and let those that have bear the burden."

This sounds more like Socialism to me than the Free Enterprise system.

The way this is going we are letting some politician in far away Washington DC decide what is equitable.

Let me ask you, do we have to pay the costs for all? Is this the reward for our hard work and savings?

If so, my contention is that we will now be in a position where we will be penalizing success rather than rewarding it.

Let's examine what I have said so far.

If the wealthy are to maintain their purchasing and investment power, it is essential that they continue to be able to invest. This is to keep pace with inflation and to maximize their return on investment. This is just as you and I would do. This is our basic protection against inflation.

Whether we are wealthy or not - this is the essence of our economy and the basis of the American Dream.

Maybe we can look at what can happen with the erosion of inflation in a more practical manner-

Let's use the "consumer price index" CPI as an example. This index prepared by the Bureau of Labor Statistics acts as a gauge or perhaps a thermostat measuring inflation. It is based on the price of a variety of consumer goods and services that a family buys during a month.

It is also used by many businesses to determine rentals, leases and employee wages. It is also used to determine Social Security recipients' annual income. In fact, a one-point rise in this index triggers an additional 8 billion or more in government spending. (Note $3 billion in 1982, today it's a hell of a lot more).

The basis of this index is the year 1967 when the dollar was worth a dollar.

Today (1982) the CPI is at a level of 1.71, meaning that if we had a dollar back in 1967 and hid it under our mattress until today (1982)- it would require that dollar plus seventy-one cents to purchase the same item that cost one dollar back in 1967. Think about it.

In 1982 nearly 50% of our government spending will go for Social Services, and if we listen to big spending politicians (not naming any one party) they wanted a whole lot more but, will you ever know where it's going or to who? Today 2022, Medicare, Social Security and Medicaid is equal to 65% of federal expenditures (this does not include the costs of those millions of illegals)

As a side note I personally am sick and tired of the politicians who we put in office trying to divide and get us to choose sides by putting the haves against the have nots, even the races and genders. Then the name calling if you don't agree with their logic or lack of. In my estimation this is just an excuse when you don't have an answer.

It's time we all be concerned about the best interests of our country, regardless of the party we side with. And certainly, punishment for hard work is no cure for our national ills.

Crisis In Our Schools

This was a talk I gave on July 27,1983, yes over 40 years ago. Things have changed in the past 40 years but, have they really? As you read this, I'll let you make that decision. Let's see, crisis is a word much loved by editorial writers and members of the media.

For those who have been around for a time, whether it be in business or the journalistic fields, the word is seldom used.

In fact, I can't remember the last time I used the word. How about you, when was the last time you used it?

However, perhaps this is going to change. The reason being that I recently read a report by the National Commission on Excellence in Education delivered to the President. (remember this report was given almost 40 years ago).

In summary the commission reported that the foundations of our society are being threatened by "a rising tide of mediocrity that is sweeping our school systems." If so, this is truly a crisis.

While my talk tonight is directed toward "articulation" and "pronunciation," (note this is what I was being judged in a speech contest) we have some 23 million American adults that are functionally illiterate. That's by the simplest test of everyday reading, writing and comprehension. Note: today 2022 the number has jumped to over 32 million or 1 in 7 Americans.

It seems the average achievement of high school students is now lower than it was 26 years ago. Wonder what that number is today and not 66 years ago? That is 1956? It was also reported that millions of dollars (1983) are being spent by the military alone on remedial education in the basic skills. Note: again, it's no wonder the military in 2022, the totally volunteer army, is having trouble finding qualified candidates with basic skills. How about businesses, after all we have 11 million job openings that are going unfilled.

What caused this deterioration?

There are several theories expressed in this summary.

Now remember this was 40 years ago. Some say the changing role of women is one explanation. Seems in past years the cream of working women were in the teaching professions since this was their only avenue. Today these women (for the most part) are in the business fields as this is where the money is.

Another plausible explanation is that the changing theories of education have lured our children away from books and to television, and now in 2022 into social media and other nonproductive pursuits.

School Boards and state governments have yielded to pressure groups with the result that we now have veered from fundamental education to other activities like driver education, sex education, drug activities and the like taking away from basic curriculum. Duh!

Time in school could be another culprit. It seems every other day the schools are either out for one reason or another or focusing on some other innocuous activity. In 1956 school averaged 210 days, today (1983) that average has been reduced to 175-180 days in session. Many of the highest-ranking countries of the world have much longer terms. For example, I just read in the LA TIMES (1983) the school term in Japan is 240 days. If the quality of education in the USA and Japan were equivalent, the amount of learning time alone would result in a 33% better education!

Crisis indeed !

What can be done to change this?

Here are a few ideas:

- State and local chambers of commerce are already active in the field of public education but are they doing enough. Check it out, they can be doing much more than just standing by. After all, look how much money is being allocated to each student's education. Trust me it's a heck of a lot more than any other country in the world by a long shot. Where is that money going? We've got to know.
- Teacher's pay is always a big issue. Teachers' unions are involved and they seem to have a great deal of control. Perhaps the way to attract the best and brightest of women and men teachers would be to base pay on "merit." That would be something new.
- Then there has been a great deal of revolt by parents in recent times and they should be more involved in the school curriculum. Many areas are revolting despite our government yielding to unions calling parents "domestic terrorists." Give our kids a break.
- At the elementary level focus on the three RRR's yes Readin, Ritin, and Rithmatic.
- At the secondary level we have what can be called a cafeteria -style curriculum in which the courses are the appetizers and desserts. Often these are mistaken for the main courses. How about upgrading the number of these classes to consider 21st century education needs?

Learning is not a venture. If we want to continue to have a competitive edge, our students and citizenry must be characterized with skilled intelligence.

Now I originally wrote most of this for a talk given in 1983. It is true that it was a longtime ago and times have changed and while I'm older, I'm not ready for the rocking chair.

Let's get back to the basics before it's too late.

Note: Most of this was written by me in 1982 in a speech. Seems like only the numbers have changed. I have included a few updates from my point of view. Here is an added note that I thought you would be interested in.

Recently I talked with someone who was associated with the public schools. I asked what he thought. His response was that it seems like I was kind of naive.

Now of course I may be naïve since I'm not involved with schools, especially on a day-to-day basis. However, forty plus years ago that was different. What has happened in that period?

Last I heard the United States ranked 38th out of 71 in the World! Forty years ago, we were number 1. It's sad that it seems high school grads can't read up to standards and math and science rankings are abysmal.

However, they are very good at social media. Oh Boy! Parents used to be an integral part of their child's education process. Now they are considered domestic terrorists by our government and the teachers union. Can you believe it?

The question is where do we go from here? Amen, enough from me.

Education

Over forty years ago I gave the previous talk entitled "Crisis in our schools." Recently I found the text of this speech in my archives and along with some updates it was included in the previous chapter.

Here is how I look at it.

First, education is something we all should have available to us. The reason is we all should be taught to think and learn as a result.

Thinking is more than the people in the early years of mankind had available to them. After all their main concern was to find a way to feed themselves, stay alive and promulgate, just like animals. You remember learning in school about the Stone Age and earlier? Right?

Again, they were only concerned with staying alive.

Then much later Socrates, Plato and Aristotle changed the world and taught us how to think. Of course, there were others before them, but they were the instigators of modern thinking and learning.

Where did we go from there? Oh, it was not a straight-line journey but the ability to think, process, access and use logic led to the many great things that not only enabled us to improve how we lived but to develop a moral clarity.

That clarity is something like doing good things for not only ours, but for all people.

For example, engineers have developed new products, systems etc. Then there is our fragile agriculture system that enables the world to be fed and prosper. How about the medical field and our ability to lead a healthy long life?

I can go on and on and here's the point, proper education and the ability to think along with moral clarity is the differential between humans and animals.

Where are we today? I would hope it is not how I perceive it as being more like in our education system "brainwashing." My question is where has the moral clarity gone?

From what it seems it is in the process of disappearing, especially in the major, elite universities and don't forget our elementary and high schools.

Then there are our elected officials that come on as being " for the people oriented" but become something else while in office. From there it's about power and getting reelected. The welfare of their fellow Americans becomes secondary even for their neighbors, relatives and friends.

Have included a short story about an incident that occurred several years ago as a youth. Hope you like.

Another Memorable Day With My Dad

It was another lesson from my Dad. You know how it always is, Dads like to teach their kids no matter how old they are.

Believe it was about late July 1961.

At that time, I was the number one pitcher on my college baseball team and number one pitcher on our Lake View semi pro baseball team. We were called "The AC's"

This year was special as our team was sponsoring an "old timers " game with retired Lake View baseball players. If we go back in time, Lake View had a semi pro team as far back as the early 1920's. They had some good teams and even won the New York State championship in 1951. A couple of the players from that team signed pro contracts with Major League teams. They had a host of real fine players over the years. This included my Uncles Al and Rich and cousin Wally. Also, my dad was among them. In the late 30s. Dad was also a super pitcher for St. Joe's High School while in school and after for the Acer's.

But now he was in his late 40s.and was selected to pitch one inning in the old timer's game. I remember his practicing to get ready and he could still bring it...

He did pretty good considering. And guess what, I got to get an at bat while he was on the mound. Now, I was known to be a pretty good hitter and was probably a bit cocky as I strolled to the plate. After all these were old timers, we were up against. I know for sure I was anxious as hell.

Now here comes the first pitch from Dad and guess what, it was aimed right at my head and knocked me on my butt. Holy Crap! Dad made sure he took me down a notch or two.

However eventually he got one over the plate and I was able to sneak a tweener tween first and second for a measly single.

I'll never forget that at bat that day. Thanks, Dad, for one of the many lessons that helped make me a man. Your humbler son Mark.

On the lighter side here is a story from my Master Gardener days. It's a story about a typical week in the life of a female gardener and her spouse.

She dug the plot on Monday. The soil was rich and fine, but she forgot to put the dinner on, so we went out to dine.

She planted roses on Tuesday, she said they are a must.

They are quite lovely, but she forgot to dust!

On Wednesday it was daisies, they opened with the sun, all pinks and whites and yellows, but the laundry didn't get done.

The poppies came on Thursday All bright, cherry red. I guess she was all engrossed as she never made the bed.

It was violets on Friday in colors she adores, it never bothered her at all the dirt upon the floor.

Saturday, I hired a maid. I'll not admit defeat. She can garden all she wants, the house will still be neat.

It's nearly lunchtime on Sunday, I cannot find the maid. Oh, I don't believe it. She's out there by my wife with her own spade.

What a week!

Did I ever tell you about my baseball stories? Probably not, so here goes. The reason I'm including this is during my youth baseball was my life. In my youth What Mattered the most was sports like baseball, basketball, football, golf, even hockey and bowling were big deals. Just goes to show you as we grow older priorities become more centered or focused. I'll bet y'all have some stories to share. Hope mine are as good as yours. Maybe, Maybe not.

Promise I'll only tell you a few. I started as a sophomore at Fr. Baker High School as a 14-year-old. First game was against Bishop Fallon H.S. Our starting pitcher was getting blasted in the first inning when Coach Stanton took him out and put me in, he had only gotten one out in the first inning, left three men on base and had given up three runs.

It was just in time as I got the other two outs and left all the runners on base. Thereafter I pitched 8 2/3 scoreless innings. We caught up and went into extra innings, I was up and got a hit, moved to second base and scored the winning run on Jerry Brokob's single.

That was my start.

After we got back to our school, I hitchhiked home and couldn't wait to tell my parents about the game. Got a big write up the next day in the Buffalo Courier Express.

But there were many others that were not so great. Another time I was getting shelled at a game against St. Joe's H. S. when Coach Stanton came out to the mound and gave me some poignant advice. He told me I can get these guys, just be more aggressive by pitching a bit more inside. Of course, I did and ended up hitting the next batter and broke his arm with my pitch. Thereafter was no problem and we ended up winning the game. Oh, not so proud of breaking the boy's arm. My bad.

Then there was the time the Bishop Timon pitcher was throwing a no- hitter against us. I was the last hitter for us in the bottom of the seventh with two outs. I had two strikes against me but ended up lining a single over second base. While I got the hit to break up the no- hitter we still lost 1 to nothing.

Then during one preseason in my second year I was in the outfield during batting practice, not really paying much attention. My mistake, as the hitter lined a drive and hit me square in the family jewels. Man, that hurt! The point is, pay attention.

I remember a game while playing for Lake View in our summer league. I was stationed in right field when the opposing hitter hit a liner about 20 feet to my right. I took a running start and made a vertical diving catch. Got a big hand from the home crowd when the inning was over.

Another time while playing left field the opposing batter hit a deep fly ball over my head. I ran back to the fence and caught the ball as it was going over the fence for a home run. Oh, that's only part of the story as the fence was a snow fence and as I jumped to catch the ball I got caught up on the fence, knocked it over and ended up tearing my uniform and getting a big slash on my hip. Oh well, still caught the ball.

While pitching one game against the Hamburg team the umpire was stationed behind the mound. He was a real nice man and a good ump. I remember him well. Unfortunately, while at bat I hit a line drive through the middle. The pitcher ducked and the ball hit the Ump in the arm, breaking it. My gosh what's with me breaking arms?

Oh, did I mention his young daughter was Miss New York State. Do you think I was reluctant to go back to the mound? Just my luck.

One year I was part of the Southern Tier All Stars team held at the Erie County Hamburg Fair. Being the starting pitcher for the Southern All Stars I got to pitch five innings. Did well after five innings, giving up NO Hits. Asked our manager if I could go the rest of the way or at least until I gave up a hit. He thought it over and agreed. Went the rest of the way and pitched the only no hitter of my career. Had a few one hitters, but this was my first No Hitter. Yes, against the Northern Tier All Stars.

The opposing pitcher was Pat Dobson. Pat later became a 20-game winner for the Baltimore Orioles and won over 100 games in the Major Leagues. Also, a renowned Major League pitching coach.

Note: In High School I was a two time All Catholic league pitcher .The other All Catholic pitchers over the two years all signed pro contracts and each made it to the Major Leagues. While I had the opportunity, I didn't sign a contract but have no regrets.

Then there was the Sunday before graduating from College.

I came home to pitch for Lake View in our opening game of the summer league. As I was warming up on the mound the infielders were doing the same. Our first baseman Carl Abramo was tossing balls to the infielders. Unfortunately, he threw one to the third baseman and threw it too low and hit me in the face just below my right eye. It nearly knocked me out. The crowd came rushing with ice and I slowly recovered. The throw had numbed the right side of my face and for the next year that side of my face was numb. Eventually it went away. However, I felt okay and decided I could start the game. I pitched the whole game, and we won!

However, my graduation pictures showed a great "black eye" not too good. The Courier Express made a big deal of it in the next morning's paper.

Here's one more high school story. During my junior year after pitching and winning a complete game against Canisius High, the coach for Canisius Mr. Connie Magillicuddy approached me and asked if I could pitch for his team in the summer AAABA league in Buffalo. I said I sure would like to, but I had no transportation to get to the games in Delaware Park. He asked where I lived and said he would be glad to pick me up and return me home before and after each game. We played both on Tuesday and Thursday at 6 pm. It was about 40 miles round trip. That was great but, hoped I would do well otherwise I might not have a ride home !

Fortunately. I did okay and won all my games except for one that we lost even though I had three hits in the game. Also hit over .500 for the season. Now AAABA was the highest ranked baseball league in Western New York. The Buffalo Evening News wrote an article about me saying not only was I a fine left-handed pitcher but one of the best hitters in the league.

Of course, I also played for my home team Lake View that summer. We also played two games per week. One week I pitched against Orchard Park. It was a hot Sunday, almost 100 degrees and humid. That day we went into extra innings. I pitched 15 hot innings, but we lost. On Tuesday at

AAABA Mr. Mac knew I had pitched on Sunday but asked if I could go - told him I felt good and yes, we won. Then on Thursday our scheduled pitcher had a sore arm and couldn't go. So, I volunteered and went another seven innings. We won again.

Then on Sunday I started for Lake View and pitched six innings. Jimmy Anderson came in to relieve me and I went into right field. Again, we went into extra innings. I came up in the eleventh inning and wouldn't you know it hit a home run over the tennis courts fence for the winning walk off run.

Now that week was something with 35 innings pitched three wins and one loss plus a game winning extra innings home run. As I think back now that I'm 82 years old, how the hell did I do it?

That week *The Buffalo Evening News* awarded me "Player of the Week" in Western New York, and I was interviewed on WGR TV.

There are many other stories, especially about my four years in college baseball. But, as promised, these were just a few. Hope you like my ramblings.

Updates

Here is the status of the several individuals previously featured in my earlier books. These individuals were unique as they were all successful then during the 2008 recession suffered setbacks.

From there each of them rebounded, dug themselves out of a hole and made it back in a graceful and exhilarating manner. That is a manner worth talking about in all my books. Their stories bear repeating and I'm so proud of all of them. I won't repeat their entire stories but just a short recap and an update of where they are today.

The first saga involves the story of a successful businessman Robert Pedregon who owned a very successful coffee shop in Costa Mesa, CA. Plus he had owned two other shops along with a pizza shop. Then six months before his ten-year lease was up, he got a knock on the side of his head.

Seems Starbucks went to his landlord and bought out his lease as they wanted the site to open their own Starbucks. He had no choice but to close his shop.

He thought about his options and at the age of 43 decided to apply to various police departments to become an officer. Now again this was during the '08 recession and not much hiring was going on. However, while it took a bit of time he was accepted by the California Highway Patrol.

Only problem, not as a uniformed officer but in the 911 office as a dispatcher. He had to go through training in Sacramento and came out as the number one recruit.

With that he was even offered duty in Sacramento as part of the Governor's elite guard. He declined that offer as his son was living with his ex-wife in Orange County and he was not going to exit his son's life.

He went back to Dispatch and kept applying to other police departments and shortly was accepted into LAPD Police Academy at their Airport division called The World Police.

Of course, he had to go through a six-month basic training class competing against twenty- and twenty-one-year-olds just out of the military.

Generally, Rob was used by the DI as an example during this time. When he beat out the rest of the recruits the DI admonished them by saying, "You let that old man beat you out?" Once when the DI, who always called him old man, said. "Hey Pedregon," Rob thought he got a promotion.

That wasn't the least of it as Rob worked at this time 24/7. Their training was Monday through Friday but on Saturday and Sunday he worked with two fellow recruits. When graduation time came, I spoke with both, and they told me that without Rob they probably would not have made it. You can read the story of their first night out in my previous books, it's very interesting.

Well, Rob did graduate and ended up as the number one academic and being one tenth of a point from being the number one cadet. He also ended up carrying the American Flag in the graduation parade and became a part of the LAPD Honor Guard. He still is today. There is a lot more, but you will have to read my other books to hear the whole story. Especially the story about the terrorist takedown that earned him and his fellow officers the Medal of Valor. As a summary along the way, he was chosen to represent LAPD in Washington for the fallen cops memorial, one of the top marksmen in LAPD, promotion after promotion, applied for and became a Motor Cop , received the MEDAL of VALOR {highest award given in California} for taking down an airport terrorist. Then was asked by the Chief to be the temporary PIO {Public Information Officer}. He did this temporary position for over three years.

There are a few other awards, but I promised to be brief in my recap so here it is, he not only became sergeant but during that time was asked to rewrite the department's policies and procedures manual. They had been trying to get this done for the past ten years. Rob got it done in less than one year.

Oh, he just received a promotion to lieutenant. That's enough for now. We are so proud of this man.

Now what about the son Austin he would not leave behind. He is now a LOS ANGELES Deputy Sheriff. Also, so proud of him, just like his dad.

There is still more, as after he and his ex-wife split, he met this young girl named Nicole at his coffee shop. She was an aspiring teacher. They have been together now for 25 years. By the way she was just named "Teacher of the Year" at her school. So proud of her also.

The next recap is of an extraordinary couple I call "The Doc and the Girl." You can also read about them in my earlier books. They have had a very interesting story. In '08 Steve graduated with his Doctorate in Chiropractic medicine. The only problem was this, the 2008 recession was in full force and for the most part new Chiropractors did not have a patient following. He was fortunate to get a practice to hire him, but they could only use him for two days per week.

This was not good enough as he had to make a living and two days per week would not make it. So, what he did was use his skills as a handyman the other days to make it. That he did, remodeling kitchens and bathrooms along with other projects.

Along the way he researched other parts of the country to see if he could find a full-time Chiropractic position.

Just so happened that he found a practice in Columbia, South Carolina that was looking for a manager/doctor. He checked it out and thought it would be a good place to get a start.

After seven years working for someone else it was time to strike out on his own.

Again, he researched around the country and found a good practice in Austin, Texas where the Chiropractor/owner was looking to sell and retire. He decided to buy the practice and move to Texas.

This is where the Girl comes in so we will tell her part of the story. Her name is Marisa and both she and Steve graduated in '08 and started their story at about that time. They had mutual friends and when they met it was almost like love at first sight.

They became a pair.

She had graduated with a master's degree in film and was looking to get started in the industry. Only problem films were not being made in Los Angeles. However, she took a position at PARAMOUNT STUDIOS hoping to make a start of her career and she did. First, she gave tours of the extensive studio lot to bigwigs and visitors, got several promotions along the way and even worked on some TV shows like Dr. Phil and Dancing With the Stars. She learned a bunch and even met some Directors and Producers. They loved her at Paramount and were very disappointed when they learned she was moving to South Carolina with her guy Steve.

So off she went without the hint of a job. However, she shortly became a networking guru and got an offer from the local Fox television channel. Columbia was considered a small market, and the channel was not owned by the Murdock group.

She loved both Columbia and her job at Fox. She became a Southern girl and both her and Steve still go back a couple of times each year to watch the USC Gamecocks football games.

You had read about her time in Columbia in my previous books and know she did some great things in the local television market.

With that she got promotions and when she and Steve moved to Austin, Texas she had three job offers before she even met the people. They knew a good thing when they saw it!

Where did she go now? It was special as she became assistant to the FOX station manager. She took that as she wanted to expand her horizons and that she did. From there every problem that came up at the station she was assigned to get it resolved.

Even in her first year in Austin she was voted by the Total Austin Women in media as the "Unsung Hero" among Austin media. This was something special as you can imagine. From there it went to greater responsibilities at the big FOX channel. A couple of years ago a 20-year veteran at the station decided to retire.

The person was in a key position as program director. This meant that in this position she was responsible for always keeping the station on air. Dead time for television is a no no. That is even when sports games like the World Series, NBA finals or the National Football Leagues games and Super Bowl exceeded their time slots.

This became a big deal, and Marisa was asked to fill this slot as acting program director. It was difficult as she had to do more than just that. She also had to do her duties as assistant to the station manager.

Seems Fox was going through financially difficult times and had to cut back on hiring.

Somehow, she was able to handle all the issues and excelled at each.

As acting director, she was even assigned to help teach a new acting program director at the Dallas FOX station how to get the job done. This meant that once or twice per month she would have to drive to Dallas and work with this new person. She really liked doing this. Just goes to show you how a person reaches their potential. Yes, from a Film mogul to a TV executive.

Now she has been promoted from acting director to actual Director. A big deal as she is in line to become a vice president of FOX in the next couple of years. Holy Crap.

Oh, there's more along the way. She became an officer of the "Women in Media" in the Austin area and is currently up for Vice President of the organization.

Probably after this President.

Steve and Marisa both showed the resiliency of what it takes to weather through both the good times and the difficult times. This is the American Dream as well as exhibiting What Matters the Most.

Our final recap involves businessman extraordinaire Greg Edwards. Greg had always been a rainmaker. That is, he made things happen at the companies he worked with. He even started his own company in the embroidery business, making logos on golf shirts and the like. It became very successful and one of the largest of its kind in the Buffalo, New York area. He had invested a great deal of money in the embroidery equipment and was greatly in debt as a result.

All was well until '08 when the 2008 recession hit. The economic conditions were bleak, and the embroidery market dried up. With a great deal of debt and no income, bankruptcy was the only alternative.

With a young family and no funds, he had to do something to fix things for his wife and kids. He did not give up and reached out to people he knew in the hospital services industry.

From there he accepted a sales position with a large company, the Compass Group, that sold services to hospitals and quickly became their top sales representative. As I said he was a "rainmaker."

After a couple of years, he was promoted to Vice President and spent a total of eight years with the company.

However, he was not satisfied and wanted to do his own thing. He knew the hospital industry backward and forward and he approached a long time High Net Worth Wall Street friend from high school and asked him if he would like to buy a company with him. His friend said, "Sure. what are you thinking of?"

Greg told him he didn't know but would do research and they would figure it out between them.

Knowing the hospital business, he thought about what services hospitals needed. He thought that valet parking was viable as it was an area where hospitals always had parking problems.

That area was growing exponentially, and he started his research and found an organization that had potential. Now Greg's friend was going to be the money man and Greg the rainmaker.

They ended up buying the company. It took awhile to get it moving but now they are one of the fastest growing companies in the state of Tennessee and Greg bought out his partner.

Greg, we are so proud of you. It is a tribute to making the most and never giving up.

Personally, I'm amazed at what these three examples have done in the past number of years. Each time I write a new book, I include in it an update on how things are going with each story. There have been no setbacks, not because I'm such a great chooser but because they are such diligent people. This is truly what the American Dream is about, and it is my honor to share their stories.

Let's get back to What Matters the Most from my perspective. Here is more.

Human Nature

Don't you ever think that it is unusual for people to not do something when they are doing it?

It's like when you say you are not worried. You only say it when you really are.

Or when you say you don't care but you really do?

These are just excuses and are part of what is known as human nature. Usually, this trait occurs when we are scared.

From what I can determine this is called by others the "destructive instinct" of humans. In other words, we probably all have it. The only thing is it probably is not what can be called normal human behavior. It is just a defensive mechanism used by us humans, basically to justify or hide our actions.

In my opinion these are both good and bad actions. Good in that it may help us for a moment or two. Bad in that it is not the truth, and we then are not being true to ourselves or others. As a result, our excuses can eventually come back to haunt us. Ugh.

The question then is if we really want to work on self improvement, that is probably almost impossible.

Kind of like we were told as kids, one lie leads to many others, so don't lie, it's easier in the long run to simply tell the truth. This is especially true if it was an everyday part of our being and our lives, a bad habit to get into.

Since this book is supposed to be a part of our dealing with change, self esteem and self image I guess we should be careful of what we say!

Yes, human nature is a very mysterious thing. But, think about it, don't most of us want to get better every day?

Guess that was part of God's plan when we were given "free will."

Using a defensive mechanism to justify our being can be a bad part of human nature. Do you ever do that? Don't feel bad, most of us do it at some time in our lives. Wish I knew how to overcome our bad instincts like this.

All I can really say is we can but not alone. What is that old saying, no man is an island.

While we need good influences in our lives, we also have something else. That is our creative imaginations. Good influences can help us set and achieve our objectives and goals as well as achieving them. They can also benefit our demeanor.

Our creative imagination can be to exercise the power of being our own hypnotist. That is if we imagine good in our minds, good will happen. Yes, we will believe it to be true.

That is if we work on it and have a good plan, being patient and consistent will enable us to successfully deal with changes and bad habits as they crop up. With that we will see our self-esteem and self image skyrocket.

Don't you think that the people we associate with can either have a positive or negative influence on us? Again, it's not just how much money we can accumulate or how much money they have, Maybe it is our mom or dad, uncles and aunts, even good friends etc. or even our own self indulgence. Oh, and don't forget we can also influence others with our behavior. Yes, we can be a good friend too.

My suggestion is to use that amazing brain to help solve problems or issues. Oh yeah that creative imagination, especially with the help of others like a mentor, pastor, minister, priest, rabbi or just a capable friend.

In the process of writing this book I ask for comments from people I trust. Amazing what is heard back. Things such as I like your stories or even how about with the stories, more of your personal input.

PS, I don't know why they would want more of my personal input, but I will try.

Believe me it's difficult to write a book of this nature. couldn't do it without the help of others like my editor Lee Pound. Often, I get probed with questions like what did you mean by that? Or maybe that phrase is inappropriate.

Oh well, they say the life of a writer is very lonely, and I can agree with that especially when the pandemic was in full force. Thank God at the time the golf courses were open and at least I can go to the driving range, maintain my social distance and beat some golf balls when at a mind block. Does it work ? Mostly yes.

Perhaps, it can be worth it if you can get your story out. Even more so if your story influences others.in a positive manner.

Lee Pound has always said everyone has a story, but not everyone tells their story. Thanks, Lee, for helping me get my stories out.

Happiness And Joy

I've been trying to figure out the differences. Have you ever thought of that, are there any? What did you think? Is there really a difference?

Let's talk about that for a few minutes.

Seems if you look both up in Webster's they almost appear to be the same. Guess it has to do with "spirit."

But is "spirit" the only thing that makes them the same? Personally, I don't think so. If I'm on to something, let's then look at them both. Yes, to me there is a difference.

Happiness to me is an on-going issue. That is, while it may vary in degree over time, it is generally in our make up and permeates our lives. We are either happy most of the time or we are something else the rest of the time.

Perhaps just less so or maybe not at all for the moment. Probably something happened in our lives to cause the difference. You know what I mean, an occurrence at work, maybe someone made us mad, a death in the family or a loved one. There can be many disappointments that impact our disposition.

Regardless, to me we are essentially a happy person and everyone that knows us sees us in that regard. You might go back and read the chapter about "attitude."

If we are not thought of by those we encounter as a person with happiness in our heart, what do they think of us anyway?

I can only speak for myself, but I like people with happiness in their heart and can only feel sorrow for the ones without that attribute.

Joy on the other hand to me also deals with "spirit" but is mostly a one-time thing. That is, joy does not seem to be with us all the time like with happiness. For example, I'm not full of joy when I have to get up from a warm bed at four thirty in the morning to do something I really don't want to do. Get me?

Here's another: when the Buffalo Bills win, I'm joyful. When they lose, I'm not very joyful. Just ask my wife. I'm a diehard Bill's fan. Can you forgive me for that?

Why the heck am I talking about this?

Here's why. While joy is an event (in my opinion) most of the time, it's not an all the time occurrence. Wish it was, as the complete opposite may be sadness. Not so good.

Here's another example of what I mean. Recently our daughter was able to visit us here in Texas for five days during the Christmas holidays. We had not been able to see her in nearly one year.

Believe me, while she was here, my wife, her mother, was full of both joy and happiness. After taking her back to the airport as she was leaving my wife's heart was filled with sadness. Thankfully it was a joyful sadness. Again, the joy and sadness were events and not an ongoing issue.

So, we get that happiness is ongoing, varying in degree. Joy is temporary and a result of an event. Can we also agree that those individuals without a happy demeanor (and I don't mean giddy) probably have other issues. Can those issues be turned around? That is, can a measure or degree of happiness be instilled in that person?

If this can be achieved, possibly the world can be changed.

After all, if happiness is an ongoing state and joy is the result of an event, the question becomes how can we achieve this state of mind?

Here's my simple solution or suggestion. Instead of focusing on the prospect of being happy all the time, strive for "satisfaction."

You see, being satisfied results in being happy. Not only that but we can determine the steps that it will take to make us satisfied. These steps may be big or small. Think about it!

As a wrap up, none of us ever have all the right answers. How can we deal with that fact?

Simply. Evaluate and learn to trust, then do the right thing.

What's Happening Today?

Before publishing my last book, *Stories of an Ordinary Man*, and one of my prior books, I was talking to a high up administrator of a major university about one of the chapters. The subject was: What's happening in universities today?

The administrator and University will go unnamed.

Seems one of the great things Colleges and Universities have always been able to convey to students is the ability to take the skills they learned in earlier education and teach them how to think and process. This is generally taught through classes that create dialogue about issues between the students and the professor.

What seems to have differed between now and then is that today in many places of higher education rather than creating a dialogue, it's a matter of choosing an issue and through dialogue, each side gets a different point of view. Now they must take the professor's side and retreat into respective corners. Those that take the other side are often penalized by the professor with lesser grades. To me that is sad and not a good thing. Strength of argument should be the deciding factor.

My suggestion is to find a college where professors stimulate dialogue, not just promote a point of view.

Just think, fifteen years ago Al Gore and the global warming {psycho's} advocates predicted that much of our coastal communities would be underwater by now. Don't think that happened. Yet! And how many of these climate advocates have oceanside homes and fly in their emission expending private jets?

It's funny while we all agree the climate seems to be changing just how much and what can be done about it are the real questions.

Just the other day I heard a so-called climate expert testifying before Congress and was asked, what is the carbon level today? He had no idea… careful of what we are being told by these experts.

Risk Taking, A Key To Good Decisions

My next topic is one I've written about in a previous book, but it's been quite some time ago and will include a few updates from my point of view.

The question is, are you willing to stick your neck out? Many of us don't think that is advisable, but I'm saying it is advisable at times. I don't know who it was that had that concept. Wish I knew as I have tried to lead my life with this in mind.

Now I don't consider myself a high achiever, just an ordinary man, but high achievers can calculate and manage risk.

It is here that many of us fail to act or just play it safe. Generally, this inaction is due to the uncertainty of doing something different from what we are accustomed to doing. Especially during uncertain times.

Give you an example, when I was doing gardening workshops as a Master Gardener, I often would ask the audience of wannabe gardeners the question: Who are experienced and who are new gardeners? The answers were always something like this, for the experienced gardeners I would tell them it would probably take them at least three weeks to learn what I was teaching them. They would ask why. I would tell them because as experienced gardeners they would always go back to their old ways.

For the newbies I could teach them in about one hour. They would ask how come? I would tell them because they were open to new ideas.

Again, during uncertain times, the lack of positive action can result in many missed opportunities that could have otherwise been realized.

Now as far as risk taking goes, inexperience is one reason people are uncomfortable in their role at taking a risk. Just think about how many times we all questioned management's decisions when major changes were incorporated at our companies? Hmmm.

Often it is the resistance to change on the part of the experienced that fuels uncertainty. Almost like well this is the way we've always done it.

Here are a few thoughts that may help in developing a new comfort zone.

- Keep open to new/different ideas. Guard against becoming attached to the way things have been done, people you associate with, even your job. That may be difficult to learn to detach yourself. To take and assess chances you must be able to let go.
- Challenging yourself all the time is one way to maintain flexibility. As a mentor of mine, the late Mel Bartholomew, famous inventor and Square Foot Gardening author and inventor, told me asking questions "is the best way." Questions like is this the best it can work? Or what else can I/we do? Suppose it doesn't work? And so on. Similarly, why and how come?
- These are good queries that open the mind to fresh thinking and help you recognize new trends that may call for changes in the way we have always done it.

- Start on a small scale, this will help you tolerate change. In other words, take small risks before you delve into the larger risks. You can also work on getting out of your zone by volunteering for a non-profit or industry association, starting your own group like a writer's group or just even a weekly coffee group that discusses various world or personal events, etc.
- If things don't work out the way you planned don't be discouraged. Just consider it a learning experience. Eventually you will build up a success record.
- When considering change or risk taking, one of the things you should consider is, What is the worst that can happen? Then map out the scenarios. If your conclusion is that the risk is too great, don't do it!

The ability to innovate and manage risk successfully is a plus for both career and life.

More To Come

There is so much more I want to talk about. Especially about what matters the most for each of us. This is a complicated subject, and I don't know if I'm the person that can determine what that is for each of us. However, Let's give it a shot.

Consider if we endeavor to live a good life. We try to do good things for others, maybe even have a spouse or significant other that we are loyal to, so we take care of their wants and needs, and they do the same for us.

Then we might even have children. They are ours whether we are good parents or not so good too. It's all in the eyes of the beholder.

There is generally only one trait that really counts. Of course, that is unconditional love.

Both ours and theirs.

What is unconditional love? Hmm. It is quite simple, just the fact that no matter what the love will always be there. Almost like no strings attached.

That does not mean there will always be total agreement or even understanding and forgiveness. Those are not the points as none of us are perfect.

Let's look at it in a different manner: would we still have unconditional love for someone who was a cold-blooded murderer or torturer or some other egregious happening?

WOW, I hope that never happens to any of you that are reading this stuff. However, it seems there are a whole lot of bad things going on in the world today. Just turn your television to the news both locally and worldwide and you will get an eye and ear full.

Do you think all these dirtbags are not loved by their mother, father, brother or sister? Maybe even a spouse or significant other, even a child of theirs.

I guess that tells you something. There will always be someone that loves us all, you guessed it ...God.

Now since we are talking about a subject we don't normally talk about: How we handle a subject like unconditional love. First part as previously mentioned it means essentially there are no strings attached. What does that mean?

Does it mean no matter what the person does that we give our unconditional love to, they can do anything they want, even hurt us badly without remorse and there are still no strings attached? No, because there are boundaries even to unconditional love. There are not a lot of them but there are a few. When I spoke to my wife about this subject, she said you are right, there are plenty of boundaries and you better adhere. Note: we have been married for almost fifty years and I at least most of the time have adhered.

These boundaries may include acts that are beyond our personal moral acceptance. In other words, if your partner or the recipient of your love expects you to do something that is unacceptable from your point of view that's a no no.

For example, what if a recipient expects you to assist in doing a bad deed?

This would of course not be healthy. Therefore, no strings without boundaries of some sort in my mind would not be healthy even if it was exhibited by a loved one or even a child.

In my mind healthy unconditional love requires communication and understanding by both parties.

Now all is not beyond hope. God will still love us and yes, He has boundaries just like we do. I did a bit of research to see examples of how this can work.

What I found was not all Saints led perfect lives, yet they turned to God as ultimately, He is the source of healing.

A Saint such as St. Augustine was known to struggle with chastity his entire life, yet he turned to God and became a Saint. Then Mary Magdalene, a disciple of Jesus was depicted as being a prostitute {note that was debunked} even more but there was no proof. Likewise. St. Max who died in 1941 was a derelict and St. Benedict with lust. They turned their lives around for the better.

We don't have to be saints to experience unconditional love, but it sure helps to be the kind of person that gives to others and earns the type of love that is unconditional.

As a conclusion to this section, I'm probably not a great expert in covering topics like this but, I've been around long enough to experience the ups and downs of life and consider myself to be blessed, probably more than I deserve with the people that have entered my existence. The next part is about a person that has done so much for others.

The Girl With The Green Eyes And A Heart Of Gold

First met her when she was twenty years old. Kind of a feisty gal who seemed to have a perky personality. She had interviewed with a couple of guys that worked for me and she got the job.

We had a department that was close-knit and frequently would share stories of our personal lives, both good and bad, As a result we all got to know each other well. Since it was a rather small department, when a birthday came up, we all often went out to lunch together or invited all to home parties.

After a year or two I got to more than admire this girl. Why, because I could see she was special and saw she had what I called "PO." {Actually potential} finally I got the courage and asked her out.

You are not supposed to do this, but I did, and I didn't regret it, not then and not now. Over time we became a regular couple, and she decided to find another job. Oh, did I say she has green eyes and a heart of gold.

After a couple of years, we got married and now it's almost fifty years later. Time goes by but, my reason for writing this is to tell her story, especially to emphasize her heart of gold, her career and the time after. It's quite a story.

For a time after leaving National Gypsum {my company} she went to work as secretary at an automobile dealership but didn't stay long as her boss was a pill. Then spent a few years with Memorial Hospital and got her introduction to the medical field.

After we got married the drive from Huntington Beach in Orange County back and forth each day to Long Beach was just too much.

She then left Memorial and joined The Orange County Hospital Council as Assistant to the President, Irv Schreck. Irv was a great guy. She loved the job and learned a lot, including how to hire and manage people.

It's now a few years later and after she got pregnant and had her first baby, we decided it would be good for her to take a break from work and concentrate on raising our newborn. A big enough job. And here is where her career exploded.

When our daughter was old enough, mom joined a group called "mommy and me." Since her religion was Jewish, and the group was at a Jewish temple, it fit right in. After a short time, she volunteered to teach art to young children. The only problem was that the Director Lisa required her to go back and get some early childhood college credits, which she did.

This is really when it all happened because as she took the classes, Lisa saw the "PO" { Potential} that I talked about earlier. You see not only did she do great at teaching art, but she was great with the parents.

Lisa took advantage of this and when new parents came into the school, she had Terry do the tours and give the rhetoric about the school.

Now Lisa was not necessarily an easy boss and Terry tells the story about when she was eight months pregnant with our second daughter, Lisa told her to sweep an area. After doing so Lisa came out and said, "Oh, you missed a spot!" If it was me, I would have said kiss my you know what!

She continued getting early childhood credits and even got her degree plus a degree in Preschool Administration .

The result was growth in multitudes. Soon the temple board was asked by the congregants to start a new segment called "Infant Toddler Care." They had an unusual name for this segment, "The Cuddle Club." This was special as they had babies requiring an additional baby to teacher percentage and guess who they asked to be the Director. Yes, Terry.

Not an easy job with thirty babies and twenty caregivers plus figuring out how to make a profit, etc. It was intense. That was not the only issue as the school was open to all categories and many of the Jewish congregants were not happy that non-Jews were coming and dropping off their babies. Guess there are always kinks in a new start up but eventually it all worked out and Terry was a hero at the Temple when they were profitable and successful.

Now eight years later, Terry's reputation in the Jewish community became well known.

Another local Temple at the time was looking for a new preschool director and they contacted Terry for an interview.

She thought about it and since it would be a career advancement opportunity agreed with enthusiasm. Naturally she got the job, I mean who wouldn't hire her if they had the chance.

Now this was a small school and over the next few years the enrollment grew from about twenty or thirty to close to one hundred. Along the way she was responsible for enlarging the facilities and getting a business plan in place to show how the growth would lead to profit for the Temple.

The Temple Treasurer was both her advocate and mentor and helped her make it through the rest of the board. He was an interesting guy, being a well-known criminal defense attorney in real life.

This was not by any means an easy task but with help she got it done. In the end the temple congregants grew, the Temple profited greatly, and they even opened a kindergarten.

This all happened over an eight-year period. She was even instrumental in starting a monthly luncheon with the preschool directors of the other Jewish Temples in Orange County. This is where they would not only get together on a regular basis but see each other's schools and discuss what worked and of course each other's parents and board problems and talk about ways and means of dealing with them. This was always a big deal.

Along with her reputation, I might say her reputation grew. She was highly respected among her peers.

Then one day into her eighth year at this Temple she got a visit from the religious director of a growing temple in South Orange County.

The lady came under the pretext of asking Terry for advice on what that temple needed to do to open a preschool. Then she asked if Terry knew of anyone that might be a candidate to be their new director? She even asked if she might be interested in the position. Now if I looked at this, I might ask is this Kosher poaching a person from another local temple?

What she was really trying to do was to see if she could entice Terry to become the director of their new preschool.

Terry came home that night and asked my opinion. Here were my thoughts: First were they her temple's competitors? she said no as they were in entirely different areas of the county. Okay that made it Kosher.

Next, what did they have in mind for this director?

She said they were starting out small, but she would have to design the school, oversee the building and construction and get the approvals from the State of California.

She didn't know much more as she had not met the Rabbi or the temple officers. All she really knew was that the temple was moving in the next year from a temporary site to a new renovated building. Evidently one of the members has committed a huge amount of money to this project.

Anyway, she decided to check it out as this was something she was itching to be involved in, especially in designing the new school, developing the curriculum and staff.

After meeting the temple dignitaries, while there were some concerns, she said, "I can do it." And she did!

Took a year to get it all put together but, on September 11, 2001 their opening day was scheduled. They had forty students and were all set to get under way.

Only one thing nine eleven took place. Even with that they did open and begin the new school year. What a kickoff!

From there it was one thing after another, both good and not so good, but the school grew from a small student body to over 120 students, a kindergarten and a staple of the community.

This included developing an "all inclusive" program for students with special needs. It was amazing to hear about how local public schools were referring students to Terry's school.

Because of this program, not all of them were Jewish. It almost became a community preschool.

The program became well known and respected and Terry and her associate from another local Jewish school often were asked to give talks to National groups that wanted to know how they went about doing something like this.

Then there was the recession beginning in 2008. Money began to dry up and the temple was going through hard times as were many of its members. Fortunately, Terry's school prospered, not without some hard work but, one day the temple treasurer came to her and said, "Terry without your program I don't know if we could keep the lights on!"

Finally, she had some medical issues and decided it was time to retire after 18 years.

She left with all in good stead and even started a foundation on behalf of the "special needs" students with a sizable donation to get it started.

This is not the end of the story. Remember she is the girl with the green eyes and a heart of gold. Yes, and the most beautiful girl I have ever seen. Oh, by the way she still is.

This is not the end of the story.

What has she done since she retired from her preschool career? Well, a whole hell of a lot if I say so myself.

You see, I'm around her every day and she does not just sit around taking up space. She does things for other people that need help.

First it was while we were still in California volunteering at an assisted living home teaching art among other things for those with memory loss, etc. at the same time for a local hospital helping guide those that were about to have major surgery. She was even depicted on the cover of their quarterly magazine with her story.

After we moved to Texas a whole other part of her story came into being. First it was volunteering at another assisted living home teaching art to the residents among other functions. Then came a whole new thing.

We live in a 55 and older community called Sun City in the community of Georgetown, Tx. It is a wonderful place with about 16,000 residents. We live in a great area of the community and have wonderful neighbors.

One day she was at one of the community swimming pools taking in some rays and talking to some of the swimmers when a lady struck up a conversation and told her about the women that were involved in a group called WHO, a group known as Women Helping Others. This has consumed her now for the past five years.

She asked what they do? The lady said they find ways to help local nonprofits raise cash to help support their organizations. She said, "That sounds interesting. I might like to be a part of a group like that."

She sure did and immediately got involved. Then lo and behold they saw the fire in her belly and asked her to be President of the group. Holy smokes what an honor.

At the time the group had about 195 members. Now they are in the 360 range and annually are responsible for donations in the $160,000 range, plus thousands of volunteer hours to these organizations along with thousands of dollars worth of essential goods and thousands of meals for the needy during the Christmas

Season. Along with all the good things they do she told me it's the venturing into a new part of life that brings new friendships that help us persevere. As we get older, we often crave and seek these.

Normally the President's term is two years but, since Covid put a hitch in everyone's gitalong, she took a second term and has now served four years.

Not a bad resume of doing things for others and making her part of the world a better place.

Just as a summary here are a few points as I See it :
- A beguiling smile and sign of independence and confidence
- She has a way with people and could as a result get people to do things, the signs of a leader
- Loyalty was always first in her book
- intuitive

She didn't always do things the way I wanted her to but, she always did the right thing.

A Knock On The Side Of The Head

Have you ever had one? Well generally it's a wakeup call to what is important. Often it makes you feel your dreams are drying up. So, let's get into it a bit and see if we can clarify this subject. If we live long enough, we all have at least one, probably quite a few more than one.

A knock can initially hurt some but, in the end may even feel good and open our minds to much better things.

Why is that, well it helps get us out of a rut and into a new track that utilizes our innovative abilities. Getting out of a rut can really help us do that.

If you recall I have written earlier on this in my previous book *What Comes Next*. That is how our mind is so amazing, even like no other, in all that has come before us and there will be none the same after us.

We are unique. Therefore, our brains can come up with things that no one else has ever thought of. Maybe we discount this proposition but, excuse me, don't we think we are special? Maybe not like Albert Einstein but as our own unique self.

I know that I have been knocked upside the head more than once and I also know that this has resulted in new things that got me out of my rut or at least a conceived rut.

Always the results have been to see a different part of my life in a different perspective. I won't put you through the agony of each as that is not why I'm here. My goal is to have you be concerned with knocks that have come your way and how you have persevered through the difficult times and prospered in the end.

Here are a few thoughts on how we can accomplish this. Plus, don't forget knocks are not meant for just us, they one day hit us all. Hopefully some of these ideas may help us and maybe others that are close to us. Believe me, giving a poignant suggestion can be a hell of a lot better than saying, "Oh I'm so sorry" on something like that.

Here's a few suggestions:
- Listen to what other people say about you. It will give you an insight of where your strengths and weaknesses are. For example, many years ago I would complain to a colleague about the quality of candidates that were coming into my office to be considered for various positions my clients were paying me to find for them.
- After complaining long enough my colleague said, "Instead of just bitching why don't you do something about it?" I choked back and said, What do you mean?" He suggested that I write a synopsis of what their biggest errors are. "I will put you in touch with a contact I have at the Wall Street Journal and see if they could use this in their Careers section," He said.
- Well, I wrote an article entitled *How to ruin an Interview*. The Journal editor loved it, and that suggestion started a whole new career for me as a writer. I wrote about twenty-five articles for the career section of the Journal and now I'm on my sixth book. Never even thought of that until it was suggested by my colleague. Sometimes it pays to listen!

- Next idea is to do something about expanding your mind. There is a great book out there that can help you do that. It's entitled, *A Whack on the Side of the Head* by Roger von Oech, PHD. Oh, the title of this chapter is a takeoff on the title of his book but there is no way that I'm taking anything from his edition. It's just something that had an impact on me and I wanted to share it with you. The book was written about forty years ago. Believe it's still in circulation. It will open your brain to innovation.
- Here's one more thought. Give it some thought but take action!
- After all, if you think it through, what's there to lose? Action takes precedence over words.

I hope you don't get too many knocks on the side of your head during your existence here on earth. When it happens in one form or another just carry on and make do. Good luck.

Summary

Never thought I'd get this done, yet here we are. It took me quite a while, particularly talking to various people of all age groups, to get an idea of what is important.

You know what really matters the most? Actually, it's YOU!

By that I mean it's what you do with yourself during the short time we have here. That is not a fantasy but reality. All you must do is think about the reality of who you want to be then put your head down and strive for it.

Most feel like I do that these include good health, family, having an objective that keeps us inspired and of course a Spirit that we can talk to and ask for help and guidance in our everyday life.

I've covered several issues probably not as a college professor but as an everyday man. I'll bet some of you have your own thoughts on each of these subjects and that's a good thing. Also hope you liked the updates and stories included in all my books.

Until we meet again best wishes to y'all.

Getting To Know Mark Fierle

After graduating from Gannon University, Erie, PA, he had a career in finance, marketing and business management, working with large national and international firms.

Later he became President, CEO and Chairman of the Board of a large privately owned multi-state service company. From there it was the career field where after a few years he formed his own executive search firm. Along the way he began writing career-oriented articles as a freelance writer for a division of the Wall Street Journal.

Along with his articles, he was recognized as Consultant of the Year for the California Association of Personnel Consultants.

He was very successful in all his endeavors. Later he became a University of California trained Master Gardener and Radio Talk Show Host on a program entitled "In the Garden."

This is his sixth inspirational book and fourth in *The American Dream* series, beginning with a co-authored book *Adapt or Perish*, based on the Darwinian theory of survival of the fittest and designed to help businesses survive in the era of change and social media.

Next *Rekindling the American Dream* included strategies and tactics to help us all restore hope during the great recession of 2008.

His third book is *Unbridling The American Spirit* and was designed to provide inspiration for us to lead a meaningful life, overcoming the tendencies of the "entitlement" society. This included the four building blocks of a meaningful life from Mark's point of view. Next was *What Comes Next* that includes key strategies and tactics to help deal with change, self image and self esteem.

Stories of an Ordinary Man is primarily a memoir of his life and writings but includes some short stories even a poem or two

All are available in both e-book and soft cover formats on Amazon. com. All of them are rated five stars.

www.ingramcontent.com/pod-product-compliance
Lightning Source LLC
Chambersburg PA
CBHW070307100426
42743CB00011B/2383